SHORT WALKS FROM
Hertfordshire
Pubs

Other areas covered in the Pub Walks series include:

Bedfordshire
Berkshire
Birmingham & Coventry
Bournemouth & Poole
Bristol & Bath
Buckinghamshire
Cambridgeshire
Cheshire
Chilterns
Cotswolds
Cotswold Way
County Durham
North & West Cumbria
South Cumbria
Dartmoor & South Devon
Derbyshire
Essex
West Essex
Exmoor & North Devon
Gloucestershire
Herefordshire
Icknield Way Path
Isle of Wight
Kent
Lancashire
Leicestershire & Rutland

Lincolnshire
North London
Middlesex & West London
Midshires Way
Norfolk
Northamptonshire
Nottinghamshire
Oxfordshire
Shropshire
South Downs
Staffordshire
Suffolk
Surrey
Surrey Hills
Thames Valley
North Wales
South Wales
Warwickshire
Wayfarer's Walk
Wiltshire
Worcestershire
Wye Valley & Forest of Dean
East Yorkshire
North Yorkshire
South Yorkshire
West Yorkshire

A complete catalogue is available from the publisher at
3 Catherine Road, Newbury, Berkshire.

SHORT WALKS FROM

Hertfordshire Pubs

Alan Charles

COUNTRYSIDE BOOKS
NEWBURY, BERKSHIRE

COUNTRYSIDE BOOKS
3 Catherine Road
Newbury, Berkshire

ISBN 1 85306 417 3

Designed by Mon Mohan
Cover illustration by Colin Doggett
Photographs and maps by the author

Produced through MRM Associates Ltd., Reading
Printed by J.W. Arrowsmith Ltd., Bristol

Contents

Area map showing the locations of the walks.

Introduction

If until now you have thought of Hertfordshire as little more than a platform for some of South-East England's major highways and towns, be prepared for a surprise. Out of sight and sound of these emblems of the modern world can be found numerous country parishes with delightful cottages, churches and village pubs. This book explores the countryside around some of these settlements and in total provides a cross-section of life and landscape in this marvellous county.

The walks range from 2 to 3½ miles in length and should take from one to two hours to complete. They are carefully chosen for their attractiveness and ease of navigation. The pubs have also been carefully chosen – with atmosphere, comfort, cleanliness, quality and price of food and drink always in mind.

With Sunday being the most popular day for walking, pubs where on that day there is either no food or only a roast lunch have been avoided. An exception to this is at Standon, where an alternative for Sunday walkers is suggested. All of the 20 pubs welcome families inside – not just in the garden. While some have a special menu for children, others offer them smaller portions at reduced prices. All have their own parking areas and most landlords are happy for customers to leave their cars there while on the walks, if they are asked first.

The walks can be followed on the well-known Landranger series of Ordnance Survey (OS) maps, which are on a scale of 1¼ inches to the mile. You will find that 16 of the walks are on Landranger 166, the remainder on 153, 165 and 167. These maps are valuable to the walker since they show public rights of way in good detail. Also of good value is the OS/Philip's street atlas for Hertfordshire, available in a cheap pocket edition. This is on a scale of 2½ inches to the mile and, in addition to showing footpaths and bridleways, gives the names of streets, farms, houses and pubs.

Those familiar with grid reference numbers can use these maps to locate the exact position of each pub. The numbers are six figures in length and appear under the heading 'Length of the walk'.

Compass bearings are given throughout the text where they are thought to aid navigation. While stiles, gates, hedgerows and woodland are subject to the will of man, bearings remain (as far as makes no difference) just as they are!

Bus routes given in the text are only those which provide reasonably frequent links to main line railway stations – which are in turn linked to London's termini. Hertfordshire County Council publish a set of four timetables giving all services (including rail) in the county. These useful volumes can be obtained from public libraries or from railway stations, bus stations and council offices.

Although the routes are short and uncomplicated, they are as prone to the effects of man and nature as any walk, anywhere. So do be prepared – with weatherproof shoes for mud and wet grass, trousers (rather than shorts) for the occasional nettle or briar, and, if you feel prone to the odd stumble over bumpy ground, a walking stick for stability!

You will not find anything more serious than this to impede your progress and I trust that the great British weather will also smile on your expedition – happy walking!

Alan Charles
Spring 1996

Publisher's Note

We hope that you obtain considerable enjoyment from this book; great care has been taken in its preparation. However, changes of landlord and actual closures are sadly not uncommon. Likewise, although at the time of publication all routes followed public rights of way or permitted paths, diversion orders can be made and permissions withdrawn.

We cannot of course be held responsible for such diversion orders and any inaccuracies in the text which result from these or any other changes to the routes nor any damage which might result from walkers trespassing on private property. We are anxious though that all details covering the walks and the pubs are kept up to date and would therefore welcome information from readers which would be relevant to future editions.

1 Croxley Green
The Artichoke

Perhaps best known through giving its name to a popular brand of writing paper, Croxley can trace its history back to the 12th century. At that time it was described as 'Crokesleyer' – a clearing owned by the Croc family. Although the Artichoke is a mere chicken in comparison, an inscription above the bar claims that 'This ancient hostelry has been servicing pilgrims and travellers since c1700'. Careful refurbishment has guaranteed this 'ancient' atmosphere – even down to the real gas lighting, the wintertime log fire and the colour of walls and ceiling.

The regular menu is subdivided into 'Main Dishes', 'Salad Bar' (which includes ploughman's lunches), 'Kids' Menu', 'Tasty Desserts' and 'Tea and Scones'. The home-made specials vary from day to day but often include chilli, curry and fresh battered cod delivered direct from Grimsby. You can have a meal from 12 noon to 2 pm and 5 pm to 8 pm, except on Sunday evening. The regular and special menus apply throughout, with the addition of a roast lunch on Sundays.

The real ales include Theakston Best and Courage Directors. Draught lagers are Beck's, Coors Extra Gold and Foster's. Gillespie's draught stout is offered, also Strongbow cider. The pub is open for the maximum time allowed – 11 am to 11 pm on Monday to Saturday and 12 noon to 10.30 pm on Sunday. Accompanied children are welcome in the conservatory or in the Parrot Room (where there was once a parrot!). Dogs may be brought inside, assuming they are well-behaved.

Telephone: 01923 772565.

How to get there: The pub overlooks The Green, which can be accessed from the A412 (by Rickmansworth School) between Rickmansworth and Watford. Buses W4/W5 and 321 between Watford Junction station and Rickmansworth Metropolitan Line station call at New Road, opposite the Artichoke, half-hourly on Monday to Saturday and the W4/W5 runs hourly on Sunday. There is a frequent rail service from Euston to Watford Junction and from Baker Street (and the City) to Rickmansworth.

Parking: In the pub's car park or along Green Lane at the start of the walk.

Length of the walk: 2½ miles. Map: OS Landranger 166 Luton, Hertford and surrounding area or 176 West London area (inn GR 069955).

A most attractive walk that follows the Chess valley as far as Loudwater. It twice crosses the river – near the start and at the turning point – and enjoys the intervening fields, woodland and lush meadows.

The Walk

From the Artichoke turn left into Green Lane, a cul-de-sac, and stay with it to its end, then continue forward between gardens along a tarmac path. When this soon meets a road, cross to a path opposite, which is signposted to the river Chess. Once clear of the gardens, this second path bears right and reveals the marvellous expanse of the Chess valley – or at least part of it. In view are the buildings and grounds of the Royal Masonic School and, among the trees, Rickmansworth and its church tower.

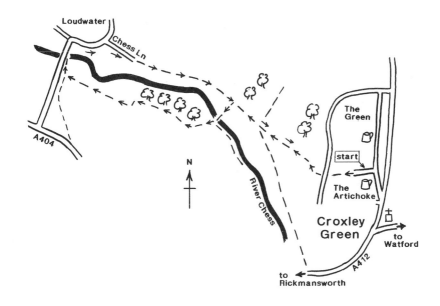

The path briefly follows a line of tall trees, then turns half-left and goes downhill to the valley bottom, where it is joined by two other paths. Go forward through a metal horse barrier here and along a path running just under the trees. After about 150 yards turn left through another barrier and soon cross the river Chess on a concrete footbridge. When you have absorbed this idyllic scene turn half-right into a path between fences, leaving the Chess behind and following a wood edge on the right. Well after the path curves right you will hear the sound of weirs on the river, and when it turns sharp left the wood is left behind. The path shortly turns right, resuming its previous direction, but now between meadows and with Loudwater's houses coming into view.

A yard or two before the path meets a road, turn right and go parallel to it before joining it. Now take care as you walk on this narrow country road through Loudwater – it is favoured by motorists rather more than you would expect. After crossing the river Chess the road turns right, then soon left by Loudwater Farm, where there is a postbox. Don't go left with the road but keep straight on in Chess Lane. Although a notice infers that Chess Lane is private, it is however a public right of way. When the lane terminates (along with the houses) a signpost and barrier leads you

Croxley Green.

forward along a footpath. You should walk between fences near the bottom edge of a meadow, although it is clear that some walkers have preferred the meadow itself, where the grass is shorter and perhaps drier.

There are glimpses of the river Chess as you proceed, and, when you reach the far end of the second meadow, an opportunity to renew its acquaintance to the full. For this, turn right through a barrier, which you will recognise from earlier in the walk. And when you are happy come back through the barrier and continue in the previous direction. A narrow path will then take you alongside the third meadow, and this in its turn to another barrier and the open valley.

You should now know your way back to the Artichoke. If not, read on! Climb the hillside slightly left (120°) and join a path running between gardens at the top. Cross a road to another path, thence through Green Lane to the pub.

② Chipperfield
The Windmill

Built, it is thought, around 1725, this outstanding country pub once served its time as an alehouse for the employees of the nearby windmill, which is now no more. Since those days it has absorbed three adjacent cottages, and now it is difficult to imagine an inn enjoying greater popularity. In summer the exterior is adorned with a remarkable display of colourful flowers, and it is worth visiting for that alone!

Every day a wide range of meals is offered, to be enjoyed in a cheerful, welcoming atmosphere. The regular menu, which includes a variety of ploughman's lunches, salads and sandwiches, is eclipsed by the impressive choice of specials on blackboards throughout the pub. One of these boards is devoted entirely to fish dishes. Others list numerous meat dishes – moussaka, ploughman's pie, honey roast ham, for example. There is also a good choice of sweets, such as cherry pie, pecan Danish and bread and butter pudding. All this from 12 noon to 2 pm and 7 pm to 9.30 pm, except on Sunday evening. Children are welcome inside (if eating) or in the garden, and can have reduced portions of any meal.

There are usually three real ales, which vary. Stella, Carlsberg and Castlemaine XXXX lagers are on draught, also Strongbow cider. The pub is open from 11 am to 3 pm and 5.30 pm to 11 pm on Monday to Friday, 11 am to 11 pm on Saturday, 12 noon to 3 pm and 7 pm to 10.30 pm on Sunday. Dogs may only be taken into the garden.

Telephone: 01923 264310.

How to get there: Chipperfield is 2 miles west of Kings Langley. It is advisable to leave Kings Langley High Street (A4251) along Langley Hill (opposite the Saracen's Head pub) and follow road signs to Chipperfield. On arrival at Chipperfield keep straight on and turn left into The Street by the Royal Oak pub. The Windmill can be found by driving along the road (a right turn from The Street) which runs past both the Two Brewers and the parish church.

Parking: In the pub's own car park or in a small parking area on the common nearby. You could, alternatively, park near the church or cricket green and walk the short distance to the pub.

Length of the walk: 3¼ miles. Map: OS Landranger 166 Luton, Hertford and surrounding area (inn GR 040015).

This route samples a few of the delights of Chipperfield's common before descending a bridleway parallel to Windmill Hill. It rises out of a magnificent valley and meets Woodman's Wood and Holly Hedges Lane. Beyond the lane the walk enjoys extensive views across elevated fields and follows a straight course back to Chipperfield.

The Walk

Turn right on leaving the Windmill and follow the road past Pill Pond (which may well be dry) to where the road changes its name from The Common to Windmill Hill. On the right you will see The Mill House, where Chipperfield's windmill (not the pub) once stood. Leave the road at this point (it subsequently starts a steep descent) by joining the second of two rough drives through the trees on the left. This is signposted as a footpath and leads to a

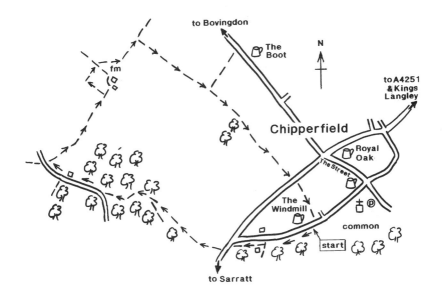

detached house, Woodlea. Turn right just before the house (not into a private drive!) along a narrow bridleway under trees. Ignore any branches in the bridleway and go straight on, then downhill to the road at the bottom.

Turn left at the road junction (into Dunny Lane) and go along this for 75 yards to a gate on the right opposite Kintyre. Climb the fieldside path – with a hedge on the right and a telephone cable overhead – all the way to a wood at the top. Go forward under the trees and eventually deeper into the wood. After the path (now a track) is joined by another on the left, it veers briefly left, then right to resume its previous direction. It is along here that the right of way has become a meandering waymarked path running parallel on the left, but almost unseen.

The path and track join forces at a bend in a narrow lane. Going forward in the lane, in due course leave the wood and pass Hollow Hedge, an attractive house on the right, then continue forward between hedges to where the lane curves right. Here you will find a pair of gates and a signposted path leading into a field. Turn right into the path and follow a succession of two field edges, with a hedge on the right along the first and on the left along the second. When you are within 20 yards of a concrete farm drive (with farm buildings and houses ahead) turn left into the adjacent field along another signposted path. Follow the right-hand hedge for about 200 yards and turn right through a waymarked gap, then follow a left-hand hedge until you meet a farm drive (a continuation of the drive seen earlier).

With the farm buildings in view to your right, cross the drive and go half-right across the next field (90°), cutting off a large corner and meeting a hedge along its right-hand border. Bear half-left with the field edge and proceed along this for about 100 yards to a footpath signpost. A tree-line coming in from the left terminates at this point. Enter the field on the right here and follow a further tree-line and scattered hedge. The glass-roofed expanse of a garden centre will be in view to your left as you now walk a straight ½ mile between the fields. From the end of this stretch a stile (initially out of sight) takes you forward into the next field. A green bridleway leaves from the left at this point, and is for those who would appreciate a short diversion to Tower Hill and the Boot public house.

Back at the stile, continue forward in the same direction as previously and enter a wood from the far left-hand corner of the field. On leaving the wood stay with the next two field edges and drop down to the road (Dunny Lane again) at Chipperfield. Cross to the stile opposite and climb a pasture very slightly right to another stile at the top. Finally walk a narrow path between gardens and turn right for the Windmill (or left for a tearoom).

3 Old Bricket Wood
The Old Fox

Not to be confused with the large village of Bricket Wood, Old Bricket Wood nestles in woodland at the far extremity of a tree-shaded lane. This delightful hamlet is the proud retainer of one of Hertfordshire's unspoilt gems – the Old Fox. Regulars, visitors and families find a warm welcome in this unpretentious country pub. They also find good food and good ale, as well as an attractive garden in summer and warm fires in winter.

The wide-ranging menu leaves little to chance. There are starters, fish dishes (Scottish smokies, smoked haddock and trout), 'Specialities' (pies, stir-fry, chicken tikka, chilli, rump steak, daily roast and much more) and vegetarian dishes. There is also a wide choice of filled jacket potatoes, ploughman's lunches, sandwiches and sweets. Children may have reduced portions of these meals or opt for their own menu. You could turn up to eat at any time between 12 noon and 8 pm on Monday to Saturday, or 12 noon to 7.30 pm on Sunday. If the weather is favourable on Sunday, the regular menu is laid aside from 12 noon to 3 pm in favour of a barbecue.

The pub is open for drinking from 11 am to 11 pm on Monday to Saturday and 12 noon to 10.30 pm on Sunday, so there is plenty of time to enjoy one of the five real ales, the three draught lagers or the Scrumpy Jack cider. Dogs are welcome inside if kept on a lead – but do bear in mind that there are other dogs in permanent residence! Telephone: 01923 673085.

How to get there: The pub can be approached from the A405 where it links with junction 6 of the M1. Initially follow signs to Bricket Wood but take care to turn left (with Mount Pleasant Lane) very soon after leaving the A405 – or risk ending up on the M1! After 1 mile and immediately beyond a railway bridge, turn right into School Lane. You will come to the pub after 1¼ miles.

Parking: At the front of the pub or along the roadside nearby.

Length of the walk: 2½ miles. Map: OS Landranger 166 Luton, Hertford and surrounding area (inn GR 126003).

Outstanding for its variety and beauty, this route samples the rural byways of Old Bricket Wood and the wooded expanse of Bricket Wood Common. It enjoys the watery delights of the river Colne and the fine vistas afforded by Munden House and its estate. Since the woodland paths and bridleways are often muddy, waterproof footwear is a 'must' for this walk.

The Walk

From the Old Fox turn left into School Lane and soon branch left into a signposted path just after a house numbered '3'. Beyond a two-cottage terrace the path passes under shrubbery and through a horse barrier, from which it joins a short drive. Go to the far end of the drive, through a kissing-gate and into a wood – Bricket Wood no less. With a field in view on the left continue forward, ignoring a stile (giving access to the furthest field corner) and a path on the left just beyond that. As the field passes from sight go forward through another horse barrier (waymarked '48') and straight on along a wide path.

Stay with the path for ¼ mile to a main crossing, resorting to a parallel path if conditions dictate. The crossing is placed between two horse barriers and is identified by a numbered waymark post.

18

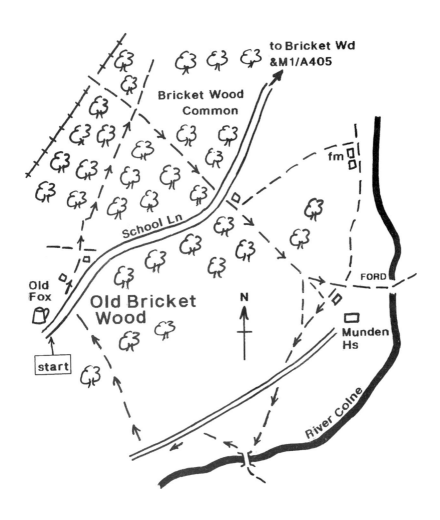

It should not be confused with a lesser, unmarked, crossing a short distance before the first of the two barriers. Turn right at the main crossing – out of '48' and into '8' – and ignore a branch on the left (crossing a ditch) almost immediately. After a further 15 yards branch left at a fork, staying in the main path (120°) and keeping fairly close to a clearing on the left. Come what may you must now continue forward in the main path, ignoring all lesser branches until, after ¼ mile, you arrive at a road.

Cross to a wide track, which is labelled as a bridleway and

The watery delights of the river Colne.

signposted 'Munden'. Go over a cattle grid very soon and continue in the track for ¼ mile to a triangular-shaped area of grass. This is backed by a farmhouse clearly dated '1880'. By passing to the left of the house you will be led down a wide track to where it fords the river Colne – a short diversion to the walk and one well worth making. In the process you will enjoy a view of Munden House, home of the 'Lord of the Manor of Bricket Wood Common'.

Back at the triangle, pass to the right of the farmhouse (its garden fence will be on your immediate left) and enter the open parkland from a stile and gate. Don't go left with the trees but cross the estate straight on along a rough drive. When this meets the metalled drive to Munden House, continue in your previous direction, but now on the grass and along a not-too-obvious path signposted to Aldenham and waymarked '4' (200°). On arrival at the river Colne once again, don't go over the footbridge (except to view!) but turn right, crossing the grass uphill (300°) back to the metalled drive.

Turning left into the drive, cross a cattle grid and continue for 200 yards to its shallow summit. Go over a stile on the right just there (numbered '2') and walk the field edge at right angles to the drive towards the mid-point of a wood. Enter the trees via a stile and keep straight on, following power lines and finally emerging at School Lane near the Old Fox.

4 Ridge
The Old Guinea

In addition to being a pleasant rural retreat, this 'sleepy hamlet' enjoys two very special associations – a terrace of attractive almshouses designed by Sir George Gilbert Scott and a churchyard containing the grave of Field Marshal the First Earl Alexander of Tunis, a distinguished commander in the Second World War.

The Old Guinea pub is popular with both local residents and visitors. Its comfortable bar connects with a separate dining room-cum-restaurant, which in turn opens out to the garden. The licensees are at pains to point out that families are welcome to use the dining room. The food choices include a good range of familiar items – lasagne, turkey escalopes, cauliflower cheese, to mention just a few typical examples. Perhaps less familiar are the balti dishes from Pakistan, made with chicken, prawns or vegetables. Meals are served every lunchtime from 12 noon to 2.15 pm (2.30 pm on Saturday and Sunday) and on Tuesday to Saturday evenings from 6.30 pm to 9.30 pm. In favourable weather a barbecue is fired-up at Sunday lunchtimes and, with the addition of ploughman's lunches and sandwiches, takes the place of the daily menu.

There are usually three to four real ales, including Benskins and Burton. Castlemaine XXXX and Stella lagers are on draught, also Red Rock cider. Tea, chocolate and three varieties of coffee are available too. Opening hours are from 11.30 am to 2.30 pm and 5.30 pm to 11 pm on Monday to Friday, 11.30 am to 11 pm on Saturday, 12 noon to 3 pm and 7 pm to 10.30 pm on Sunday. Dogs are welcome inside, but in the bar area only.

Telephone: 01707 642126.

How to get there: As the crow flies, Ridge is only ¾ mile from the A1(M)/M25 junction, but access from there involves a complicated series of roundabouts and requires the assistance of an able navigator. Better to approach from the B5378 St Albans to Borehamwood road at Shenley, along Rectory Lane (by the Black Lion pub). Turn right at the T-junction after ¼ mile and very soon left into Mimms Lane (signposted to South Mimms), then turn right into Deeves Hall Lane after a further 1¼ miles.

Parking: In the pub's car park or along the roadside nearby.

Length of the walk: 2¼ miles. Map: OS Landranger 166 Luton, Hertford and surrounding area (inn GR 215004).

So near to the M25 and A1(M), yet so much apart; a walk into the depths of unspoilt Hertfordshire, with its fields and woodland, its watery field margins and oases and its flowery hedgerows – and some of the best views in the county!

The Walk

From the Old Guinea make your way to the village green nearby and join a rough drive (signposted to Rabley Green and Shenley) running along its border. On entering the churchyard the grave of the First Earl Alexander of Tunis can be seen to the right, under a sycamore tree. Passing to the left of the church, look for a stile in the left-hand hedge. This is about 20 yards prior to the far left-hand corner of the churchyard and provides access to a field. Cross the field while aiming for the point where power lines appear to converge, well to the right of a house with three prominent chimneys (270°). Go over a stile there and continue straight on in

St Margaret's parish church.

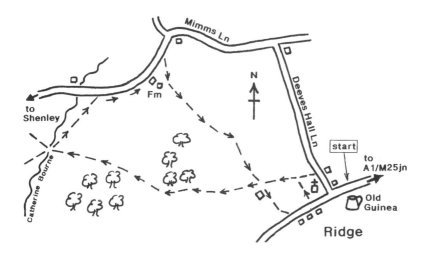

another field to a stile. This is adjacent to a small pond – in the summer a little haven of wildflowers and butterflies.

Keep forward across a meadow to its far right-hand corner, passing under electricity wires as you go, after which keep more-or-less straight on along a field edge, with woodland on your immediate right. A stile at the far end of the wood will connect you with a field on the right, which you should cross diagonally, aiming for a stile at the right-hand extremity of another wood (290°). Having clipped the corner of the wood, continue straight on and downhill to a dip where the fields meet, enjoying the marvellous view as you descend. The Catherine Bourne flows along the dip and waters a pleasant oasis between the fields.

Once in the dip turn hairpin right into a long, narrow field, with the bourne on your left and a ditch and hedge on your right. Walk approximately midway along the field (40°) and make your exit through a gap at the far end. Turn right in the road (the bourne passes under the road about 50 yards to the left) and follow the road uphill and past Ravenscroft Farm to a stile on the right. The stile appears in the hedge about 100 yards prior to a road junction (a postbox is sited at the junction) and sets you on your way along a field edge, with a fence and meadow on the right and Ravenscroft Farm beyond that.

After passing an electricity pole and entering a wide gap (between the fence corner and a hedge) go ⅓-left and uphill through

Almshouses at Ridge.

the fields (130°). If you aim at a pair of electricity poles sited in a tree-gap on the distant hilltop, you cannot go far wrong. This route skims the right-hand extremity of a hedge (marked by a tall oak tree) and continues up to join another hedge, at its corner. With this second hedge on your right keep forward until you see a stile on the right – the one met earlier in the walk.

Bypass both the stile and the garden of a nearby house and turn left from the field corner. You will find another stile (of sorts) on the right about 25 yards from the corner. Once over the stile, cross a meadow to another stile, aiming to the right of a series of cottages. Turn left in the road and make your way back to the Old Guinea, enjoying all the cottage gems (including the almshouses) as you go!

5 Cow Roast
The Cow Roast Inn

Albeit in close proximity to three historic highways – the Roman Akeman Street, the Grand Union Canal and the London and North Western Railway – the Cow Roast Inn enjoys a relatively quiet existence, with much of today's road traffic transferred to the new A41. The site of the inn was a regular stopping-off point for cattle drovers en route to London. It has been said that the drovers would reduce their complement of cattle by one, roasting it on the spot! However, the inn's previous name 'the Cow Rest' has a completely different connotation!

The menu card introduces itself as a 'seasonal selection of the best of English cooking' and includes steak and kidney pudding, roasted Aylesbury duck and fish and chips with mushy peas. Very English indeed! The separate blackboard menu offers 'Lite Bites' – sandwiches, jacket potatoes, ploughman's lunches and Cow Roast Specials, while the sweets menu is something you cannot ignore! Children are welcome inside and have their own bill of fare, which will entertain as well as satisfy. Having eaten, they will doubtless make a beeline for the play area in the garden. Food is served every lunchtime from 12 noon to 2.30 pm, Tuesday to Saturday evenings from 6.30 pm to 9 pm and Sunday evenings from 7 pm to 9 pm. There is a full menu throughout. Senior citizens and children under 10 can take advantage of certain special offers on food prices.

There are usually four real ales and three draught lagers. Gaymer's cider and Guinness are on draught too and there is a good choice of Australian house wines. Opening hours are from 11.30 am to 3 pm and 5.30 pm to 11 pm on Monday to Saturday and 12 noon to 10.30 pm on Sunday. Dogs are not welcome inside, but are compensated by a bowl of water outside!

Telephone: 01442 822287.

How to get there: The Cow Roast Inn is easily found – on the A4251 (previously the A41) between Northchurch and Tring. Buses 501/508 from Hemel Hempstead station stop here half-hourly Monday to Saturday (only). There is a frequent rail service from London (Euston) to Hemel Hempstead on these days.

Parking: In the Cow Roast's car park. You may, alternatively, find a space along the lane a short distance into the walk.

Length of the walk: 2½ miles. Map: OS Landranger 165 Aylesbury and Leighton Buzzard or Explorer 2 Chiltern Hills North (inn GR 958103).

After crossing both the Grand Union Canal and the railway, the walk twice traverses the Bulbourne valley. With its fields, meadows and woodland the beauty of the valley is revealed throughout, and near the halfway point the wooded heights of the Ashridge Estate and Aldbury Nower can be enjoyed from afar.

The Walk

From the Cow Roast Inn cross the main road (the A4251) with great care to the unmarked lane opposite and go with this over the canal bridge. Turn right with the lane and follow this for just 120 yards to a stile on the left. Cross the field here at right angles to the lane, aiming for the railway footbridge. Once over the footbridge, continue forward across the next field to a gap in the tree-line opposite. Turn left from the gap and walk the straight track

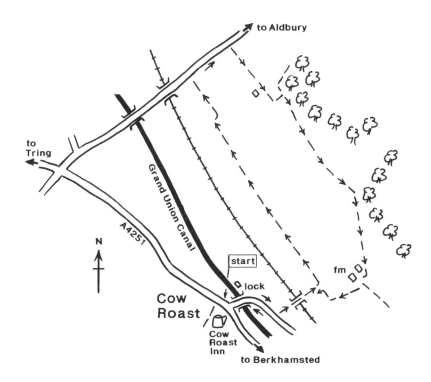

between fields, with the tree-line now on your left. The track eventually curves right by tall trees, and soon left, resuming its previous direction but now along a right-hand field edge. The track climbs a little and joins a lane from the far right-hand corner of the field.

Turn right in the lane and soon enjoy a view across Aldbury village to the woodland at Ashridge. A bridleway signpost on the left after 200 yards is your cue to leave the road for a farm track on the right. After passing a barn go through a wooden gate and into a field. The next port of call from the gate is a stile in the top left-hand corner of the field, but the right of way to this is firstly forward for two-thirds of the field length, then left across the field to a wood edge and signpost, then right along the field edge to the stile. A complicated way to cross a field if ever there was!

Cross the next field diagonally to a stile (not in view at the start) about four-fifths of the way along the right-hand field edge (160°).

Cow Roast Lock.

From the stile go down through a scrubby patch, turning left in the process and soon entering a cultivated field at its corner. Keep forward here by following the field edge, with a hedge and trees on the left. The path runs into a dip and bypasses an impressive swathe of pastureland. It then heads up towards tall trees and a stile in the top left-hand field corner. The graceful footbridge crossing the road carries the Ridgeway Path, a long distance trail from Ivinghoe in Buckinghamshire to Overton Hill in Wiltshire.

Cross the next field diagonally towards the left-hand end of a long, grey barn (180°) and enter a farmyard from a stile (there is a farmhouse directly ahead facing the yard). Go left along a rough drive for a few yards only and branch hairpin right into a track. Passing the garden of the farmhouse, soon bear left from a stile and gate. Turn right in the track after about 100 yards (not straight on to the silage heap!) then left through a hedge gap after a further 100 yards. You have now completed the loop, and all that remains is to tread the first part of the walk in reverse order. For this, cross two fields – interrupted by the railway footbridge – and turn right into a lane, following this back to the canal and the Cow Roast Inn.

6 St Albans
The Six Bells

At the end of the 19th century St Albans could boast no less than 90 hostelries. It is now down to a mere 50 or so! Among the survivors is the Six Bells, situated in one of the most attractive streets, and the only public house within the bounds of the old Roman city of Verulamium. A panel in the dining area details the discovery, in 1974/5, of an early Roman bath building when an extension to the pub was in progress.

The regular menu at the Six Bells lists starters, baguettes, ploughman's lunches, main meals, children's meals, sweets and beverages. Examples of the main dishes are lamb rosemary, chicken, ham and leek pie, vegetable lasagne and omelettes. The daily specials on the blackboard could include harvest vegetable bake, breaded scampi, macaroni cheese and a further choice of sweets. A full menu is offered every lunchtime from 12 noon to 2.30 pm (4 pm on Sunday) and Tuesday to Saturday evenings from 6 pm to 9 pm. A roast lunch is additionally available on Sunday.

There are usually five real ales – four regulars and a guest, which

varies. Addlestone's cider and Guinness are on draught, as are Castlemaine, Lowenbräu and Skol lagers. The pub is open from 11 am to 11 pm on Monday to Saturday and 12 noon to 10.30 pm on Sunday. Children are very welcome inside if dining. Dogs should ideally only be taken into the garden.
Telephone: 01727 856945.

How to get there: The pub is in St Michael's Street and is best approached from the nearby A4147 (previously the A414) where it passes the Roman Theatre. If you are driving south along the A4147 you can turn left into St Michael's Street. If driving north, there is 'no right turn' at this point and you must make a U-turn around the A4147/A5183 roundabout after a further ¼ mile. There is a frequent service to St Albans City station from London (Thameslink) every day. Buses 300/314/330/340 link the station to St Michael's Street hourly every day; otherwise it's a 1½ mile walk!

Parking: In the pub's own car park or in the inexpensive pay and display car park nearby. Access to the latter is by turning right (if approaching from the A4147) between the museum and St Michael's church.

Length of the walk: 2½ miles. Map: OS Landranger 166 Luton, Hertford and surrounding area (inn GR 137074).

A walk through one of the county's most attractive and interesting public parks. En route can be seen the abbey church of St Alban's, the walls and south-east gate of the Roman city of Verulamium and a surviving Roman mosaic and hypocaust. Children will certainly enjoy the lake and the ducks, while those wishing to make the most of their day could include a visit to the Roman Theatre, the Verulamium Museum or Kingsbury Water Mill.

The Walk
On leaving the Six Bells go right in the road (St Michael's Street) and first left by the museum. As you approach St Michael's churchyard a short diversion towards the car park will give you sight of the foundations of a Roman basilica – 'the Hall of Justice of the Roman town of Verulamium', part of an administration

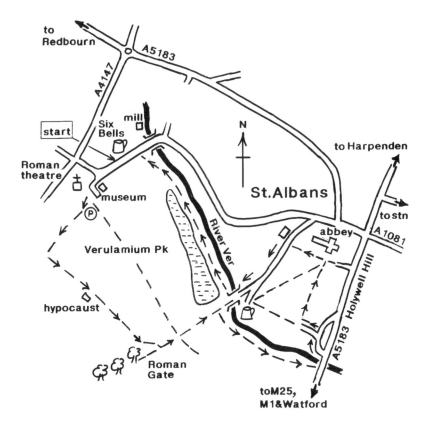

complex that extends under St Michael's church.

Entering the churchyard, take the main path and branch left into a narrow, sunken path after a few yards. Soon leave the churchyard through a gate (not into the private garden nearby) and enter Verulamium Park at its lowest corner. Turn right immediately and walk the wide path along the border of the park. Leave the path when it breaks through the hedge on the right and continue straight on along the grass – slightly uphill and with trees on the right.

Look for a brief interruption in the slope of the park – marked by a line of tall trees – and turn left there, following the trees in the direction of what at first sight has all the appearance of a bungalow. On arrival at the 'bungalow' you will discover that it houses an outstanding Roman mosaic and the remains of an underfloor heating system (a hypocaust). The building is open every day and admission is free.

St Alban's Abbey and Verulamium Park.

Continue straight on from the tree-line (in the same direction as previously), crossing the wide expanse of grass and enjoying what is without doubt the finest view of St Alban's Abbey. On reaching the tall trees opposite turn left and aim for a fenced enclosure on the right; here you will see the foundations of the south-east gate (the London Gate) of Roman Verulamium, through which Watling Street entered the city. Also to be seen is an extensive arm of the city wall.

Go down from the Roman gate, along a tarmac path and over a signposted crossing. Passing under arching trees along what becomes a raised path, walk only as far as a waymark post. This is a few yards prior to an outflow, where water passes under the path from the nearby lake. Descend the steps here and soon enter another expanse of grass, after which follow the tree-shaded river Ver all the way to a footbridge and the road at Holywell Hill. The unusual waymark arrows along this stretch refer to the 15 mile Ver-Colne Valley Walk which extends from Redbourn to Watford.

Turn left into Holywell Hill (not a hill at this point) and soon left (Grove Road) by the Tap and Spile pub. Look for a path on the left just before Abbey JMI School and follow this under tall trees and out onto the grassy slope below the abbey. Turn right immediately and go uphill on a tarmac path alongside a fence and towards the abbey, ignoring a left-hand branch en route. At the top you will find the new Chapter House. This was built on the well-excavated site of the original monastic chapter house and opened by the Queen in 1982. The abbey's bookshop and gift shop are here, also a refectory. If you are in need of sustenance at this stage of the walk, you could hardly fare better!

Turning left at the top, walk alongside the abbey (which will be on your immediate right) and straight on to the Abbey Gatehouse. Along with the abbey, the gatehouse is all that's left of the Benedictine monastery founded here in AD 793. The monastery's many other buildings were destroyed following the Dissolution of 1539. Go downhill in Abbey Mill Lane to the river Ver (you can take either of the two branches when almost at the bottom) and there find Ye Olde Fighting Cocks. According to the *Guinness Book of Records*, this is 'a foremost claimant' to the title of Great Britain's oldest inn. Cross the river by the footbridge and turn right, then walk between the river and Verulamium Lake. When the river eventually veers to the right, continue straight on to St Michael's Street.

Before returning to your car, a visit to the nearby Kingsbury Water Mill will finish your day nicely. Containing much of its original machinery, this 16th-century mill is highly regarded for its historic interest – as is the restaurant for its waffles! The mill and restaurant are open daily except Mondays.

Letty Green
The Cowper Arms

In its earlier guise as the Railway Tavern the Cowper Arms doubtless satisfied the temporal needs of passengers using the former Welwyn to Hertford branch railway, which had a station close by. Three miles of the trackbed is now the Cole Green Way, a route for walkers, cyclists and horseriders. In its superb country setting the pub is today very popular with passing motorists and those exploring the Way.

This is a Brewers Fayre pub and uses a regular menu that is found in all of its branches. Included are appetisers, fish dishes, chicken dishes, hot platters, light bites and sweets. In addition there is a separate list of daily specials. Children have their own colourful Charlie Chalk menu and they can eat anywhere in the restaurant area, which is away from the bar and smoke-free. Meals are available 'all day' every day (11.30 am to 10 pm Monday to Saturday, 12 noon to 10 pm on Sunday).

The real ales include Boddingtons, Flowers and (occasionally) Old Speckled Hen. Heineken, Heineken Export and Stella lagers

are on draught and there is a good choice of wines from Australia and New Zealand. Opening hours are the maximum possible – 11 am to 11 pm on Monday to Saturday, 12 noon to 10.30 pm on Sunday. Dogs on leads are welcome, but in the garden only.
Telephone: 01707 330202.

How to get there: The Cowper Arms can be approached quite easily from the A414/B195 roundabout midway between Hertford and Hatfield. Take the branch signposted to Cole Green and on arrival at the green turn right into the road signposted to Letty Green.

Parking: In the pub's own car park or in the Cole Green Way car park nearby.

Length of the walk: 2½ miles. Map: OS Landranger 166 Luton, Hertford and surrounding area (inn GR 284112).

Commencing with a mile of the Cole Green Way the walk enters the depths of the countryside while enjoying a mosaic of trees and shrubs. A quiet lane continues the circuit to Staines Green, and a field path to Birch Green. A magnificent valley takes over – ushering in the conclusion to this fine walk.

The Walk
Turn left on leaving the Cowper Arms and immediately go uphill on the metalled drive to the 'Cole Green Way Car Park and Picnic Area'. At the top you will be on the site of Cole Green station. Apart from the trackbed, the only recognisable feature is the station platform, cars now standing where passengers once waited. As explained on the information board, the line ran from Hertford to Welwyn Junction and was finally closed in 1966. In 1974 part of the route was acquired for recreational use and given this new name – the Cole Green Way.

You could either join the trackbed straight away or later on from the far end of the picnic area. It is then simply a matter of following the track for a little under 1 mile, ignoring the first road (which passes under the track) after ½ mile and calling a halt at the second. The bridge over which this second road crosses is in-filled and to continue, you will need to climb the slope or the steps. Turn left and

The Old Curatage, Birch Green.

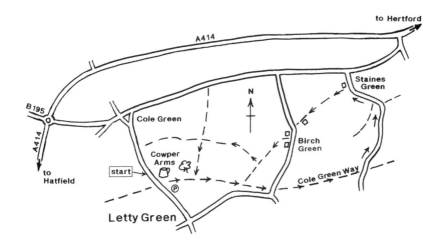

follow this quiet road in and out of a dip, going left with it at the top.

Ignore the first signposted footpath very soon on the left and continue to the second. This is about 100 yards prior to the T-junction (and 50 mph limit sign) at Staines Green and leaves the road as a track alongside the garden of the Red House. Stay with it as it crosses the fields – between fences and in the company of overhead wires. After descending a few steps at the far end of the track continue forward on a narrow path just under the trees. The fine timber-framed house in view half-left (The Old Curatage) heralds your approach to Birch Green, and the path soon places you on the green itself.

Go forward to the road and join a short metalled drive to the left of a fenced electricity sub-station. When the drive soon turns left continue forward across the fields, following overhead wires and not stopping until you arrive at a ditch and crossing at the lowest point. Turn right and follow the ditch along the dip of this marvellous valley. When after ¼ mile the track crosses the ditch turn left and go uphill in the field to a stile at a wood corner. Keep forward under the trees and soon rejoin the Cole Green Way picnic area; alternatively, take the path which loops round to the left and enjoy the prospect of a reinstated woodland pond.

Turning right into the picnic area soon go down the metalled drive back to the Cowper Arms.

8 Hertford Heath
The Silver Fox

On its run through Hertford Heath the B1197 fortunately makes use of only ¼ mile of the Roman Ermine Street, leaving the rest for us to enjoy! The Silver Fox lies close to where the two ways part company and is one of the most popular pubs in the district, Sunday being a particularly busy day here. If the weather is kind you will find that the garden, with its fountain and well-kept borders, is a most pleasant place to take refreshment. If it is not so kind you will be equally happy in the comfortable bar or dining room.

The wide-ranging lunchtime menu should satisfy all comers, including vegetarians. Examples are ham carved from the bone, deep fried scampi and vegetable lasagne. In addition to two or three home-made daily specials there is a choice of steaks, filled jacket potatoes, ploughman's lunches, sandwiches and 'splits'. And to round off the meal you have in the region of a dozen sweets to contemplate! Meals are available every day of the week from 12 noon to 2 pm and 6 pm to 9.30 pm (9 pm on Sunday). At Sunday lunchtime you can choose from jacket potatoes, salads and a variety of roasts.

There are usually about six real ales and three draught lagers (Carlsberg Export, Castlemaine XXXX and Labatt's). Draught cider is Olde English. Opening hours on Monday to Saturday are 12 noon to 2.30 pm and 5 pm to 11 pm (5.30 pm on Saturday). On Sunday the times are 12 noon to 3 pm and 7 pm to 10.30 pm. Families are very welcome here. Dogs are not allowed inside but may be taken into the garden.

Telephone: 01992 589023.

How to get there: Hertford Heath is on the B1197 and is signposted from the A414 at Hertford (Chelmsford and Hoddesdon direction). The Silver Fox lies on the B1197 and is easily found. Bus 392 runs hourly on Monday to Saturday (only) from Hertford bus station. There is a frequent rail service to Hertford East (which is near the bus station) from London (Liverpool Street).

Parking: Since the pub's own car park is quite small, you are asked not to leave your car there while on the walk. Woodland Road nearby is a suitable alternative. For this turn left on leaving the pub, then first right.

Length of the walk: 3½ miles. Map: OS Landranger 166 Luton, Hertford and surrounding area (inn GR 349111).

A walk into history and into the wealth of Hertfordshire's natural beauty. It commences with ¾ mile of the Roman Ermine Street and enters Roundings wood, part of the Hertford Heath Nature Reserve. It returns to Hertford Heath across a superb chequerboard of fields and along the quietest of country lanes.

The Walk

Turn left from the Silver Fox and left again into a rough drive just beyond the petrol station. This drive is the continuation of the Roman Ermine Street after its passage through Hertford Heath as the B1197. It soon passes Heathbury Farm, narrows to a path and enters a wood (Roundings), where an information board tells you about the wood and Hertford Heath in general. Included is the fact

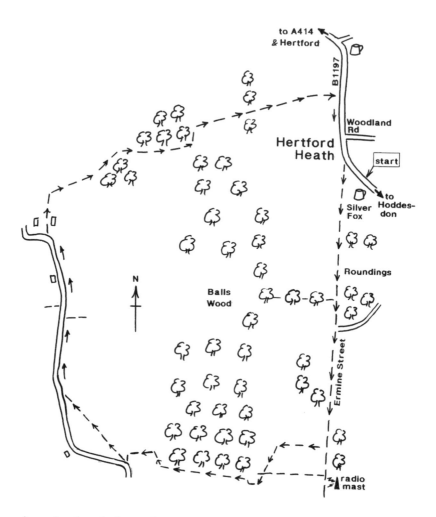

that the heath is 'a fascinating mosaic of woodland and open heathland which is now very rare in Hertfordshire'.

Keep straight on through the wood (as far as the meanderings allow), ignoring all branches and in sight of a meadow on the right. When the path evolves into a straight track and leaves the wood, ignore a gate on the right (giving access to Balls wood) and continue straight on. After a further 100 yards a metalled road comes in from the left and terminates. Keep forward here along a wide track and feel very much as the Romans felt when en route to London.

Now don't go that far yourself but continue for ⅓ mile only – until you are within 100 yards of a massive radio mast (before it, not after it). A stile in the hedge on the right is the first of eight taking you across a sequence of five fields to the distant trees. The route is at right angles to Ermine Street across the first field, then half-left (220°) over successive fields. It crosses two farm tracks in the process and passes briefly under the trees to a field. Turn right to the field corner then left to follow the wood edge.

Stay beside the wood all the way to the far right-hand corner. Go over a stile there and join a narrow path under trees. Soon cross a ditch and turn left, following a field edge, with the ditch and a hedge on the left. Cross another ditch at the far end of this field and turn left, aiming for, but not crossing, a stile by the road after 50 yards. While remaining in the field turn right and cross it corner to corner (320°) towards a shallow dip in the fields and a slim, latticed, electricity pylon.

On meeting the road once again turn right and follow it past the grand entrance to Freedom Farm and the less grand entrance to Brickendonbury, now the home of the Malaysian Rubber Producers Research Association. When the road turns left continue forward over a stile into a short path, with a fence and farmyard on the right. Soon join a farm track and continue forward again, en route to a dip in the fields. Turn half-right from the dip, crossing a field from corner to corner in the direction of a wood. Go through a gap in the far corner and follow a field edge, with the trees on your immediate right.

On arrival at the next field corner bear right towards another wood, and soon cross a footbridge to the field beyond. Keep left and follow the wood edge, eventually turning sharp left with it and stopping after 70 paces (60 yards). A waymark post now directs you into a right-hand turn, across the field towards the mid-point of a magnificent line of black poplar trees (70°). Having passed through the trees, enter an irregular-shaped field and stay with its left-hand edge all the way to the B1197. Turn right in the road and soon have the welcome sight of the Silver Fox.

Harpenden Common.

9 Harpenden
The White Horse

In its attractive residential setting, this beautifully refurbished and extended 16th-century pub overlooks Hatching Green, close to Harpenden Common. The furnishing throughout the pub – in the bar and in the dining areas and restaurant – is clearly focused on the comfort and pleasure of the customers.

The main blackboard menu includes sandwiches and baguettes, filled jacket potatoes, ploughman's lunches, salads and hot meals. Daily specials are listed separately, as are sweets and a children's menu. Food times are 12 noon to 2.30 pm and 6.30 pm to 10 pm on Monday to Saturday, 12 noon to 2.30 pm and 7 pm to 10 pm on Sunday. There is a full menu throughout these times, with the addition of a roast lunch on Sunday. Families are welcome here, and may dine in the 'TV Room' or in the restaurant. Dogs on leads may be taken into the garden or the bar, but not into the dining areas.

There are usually five real ales – four regulars and a 'guest'. Strongbow cider and Stella and Heineken lagers are on draught. Opening hours are 11 am (11.30 am in winter) to 3 pm and 5.30 pm

to 11 pm on Monday to Saturday. Sunday hours are flexible, typically 12 noon to 4 pm and 7 pm to 10.30 pm.
Telephone: 01582 713428.

How to get there: The pub is in Redbourn Lane (the B487) a short distance from its junction with the A1081 on Harpenden Common. Harpenden railway station is 1 mile from the White Horse. Trains from London (Thameslink) call at Harpenden frequently every day. Bus 307 links the High Street (a short walk from the station) to the White Horse and runs hourly on Monday to Saturday (only).

Parking: In the pub's car park or alongside the green.

Length of the walk: 2¼ miles. Map: OS Landranger 166 Luton, Hertford and surrounding area (inn GR 135130).

A walk along the attractive drives and bridleways of the Rothamsted Estate – home of the Institute of Arable Crops Research. There are superb avenues of mature trees between experimental fields, a view of Rothamsted Manor and, along Harpenden's West Common, a number of fine houses and cottages. This walk is guaranteed dry under foot except where it crosses a pasture. Here, after rain or dew, you may be glad of a pair of 'wellies'.

The Walk

On leaving the White Horse join the road that cuts through the centre of the green. This soon meets Rothamsted Park Lodge and launches you into a drive under an avenue of trees, with the Central Science Laboratory at the start. After ½ mile another drive leaves from the right, and a footpath from the left. Ignore these and continue forward for just 30 yards to a gate and bridleway signpost on the right. Cross the field here ¼-right, aiming at the far corner and skimming a fence corner as you go (320°). Two gates and a metal signpost will come into view when you are almost there.

From the gates there is a view of Rothamsted Manor and its outbuildings. The manor is in the main 17th-century, but has parts dating back to an earlier period. John Bennet Lawes was born here in 1814. In 1843 he founded what has become the oldest and most

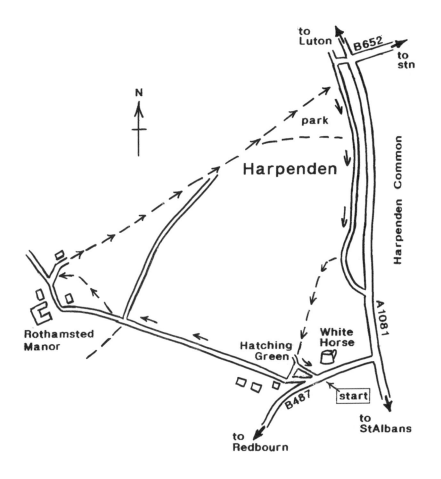

famous agricultural research station in the world and it is all around you!

Turn right from the gates and, soon passing a pair of estate cottages (including Elm Cottage), follow the straight bridleway between fields until it meets a wide metalled path. There are bridleway and footpath signposts at this point and a mounted map of the estate. Go forward along the metalled path, soon passing between concrete bollards and ignoring lesser paths leaving from the right. A fine avenue of lime trees now escorts you straight and true to the park entrance gates.

There is an opportunity to relax in a rose garden before leaving

Hatching Green.

the park, and, having left it, another to go shopping in Harpenden! But to continue on the walk (there's ⅔ mile to go) turn right from the park entrance and walk the pavement past the fire station, the Silver Cup pub and an entrance to the Rothamsted Experimental Station. Keep straight on until you arrive at a superb terrace of cottages. This is Pimlico Place, with a central plaque dating the cottages at 1822.

Turn right into a footpath a little beyond the last cottage where the road curves left. The path passes a pair of thatched cottages end-on and soon enters a field, at a corner. Follow the field edge, with a hedge on the left, all the way to the far corner, and there make your exit to Hatching Green.

Church Lane, Kimpton.

10 Kimpton
The White Horse

Nestling in a deep valley along one of Hertfordshire's narrowest B roads, Kimpton hides many of its old cottages from the passing motorist. These jewels are set around The Green and along Church Lane. The attractive 16th-century White Horse pub is less modestly placed – in a prominent position along a lively high street. The inn is noted for its comfort and the warmth of its welcome, a welcome offered to all comers, including families.

The bar menu includes a good variety of meals: chilli con carne, scampi and omelettes being typical examples. There are also ploughman's lunches, pizzas, burgers and filled home-baked rolls. A separate restaurant menu provides even more choice and is ideal for those wishing to make their visit an occasion in itself. Meals are served every day except Monday from 12 noon to 2 pm and 7 pm to 9 pm, with a full menu offered throughout.

There are usually five real ales on handpump, in addition to a 'special', which varies. Stella, Foster's and Hartsman lagers are available, also Scrumpy Jack and Strongbow ciders. There is a

choice from about 20 different wines, including alcohol-free varieties. Opening hours are 12 noon to 2.30 pm and 6 pm to 11 pm on Monday to Friday, 12 noon to 4 pm and 6 pm to 11 pm on Saturday, 12 noon to 4 pm and 7 pm to 10.30 pm on Sunday. Dogs are not permitted inside the pub.
Telephone: 01438 832307.

How to get there: Kimpton is on the B652 3 miles north-east of Harpenden, from where it is clearly signposted. The B652 leaves Harpenden as Station Road; it is then interrupted by the B653 before becoming a 3-mile-long narrow lane to Kimpton.

Parking: In the pub's car park or along the High Street nearby.

Length of the walk: 2 miles. Map: OS Landranger 166 Luton, Hertford and surrounding area (inn GR 178183).

After exploring the delightful green and Church Lane, the walk makes its gradual ascent out of Kimpton along a series of fieldside paths. It enjoys impressive views across Hertfordshire before descending open fields and joining Kimpton's churchyard path.

The Walk
On leaving the White Horse turn right into the High Street and first right into Church Lane. This will take you past the delightful green to Corner Shop Cottage. Go right with the road and soon left by the church. When the road terminates take the short path between houses (to the left of Lane End) and turn right after reaching the end of a brick-built garden wall. Cross a rough drive by passing through a pair of gates (the drive gives access to the car park of a recreation ground) and go straight on along the left-hand edge of a meadow.

Go over a stile in the far left-hand corner of the meadow and keep forward along a field edge, with a wood on the immediate left. Great care now required! When the wood is left behind stay with the field edge for 120 yards only. That's about 150 man-size paces and until you are in line with another wood edge well over to your right. Turning right from this point along a field path, aim for the edge of the wood and a white-painted house, and eventually join a road. Turn right in the road and soon left beyond the white house,

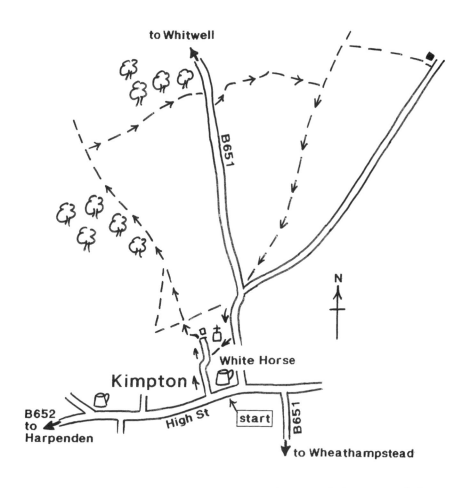

along a path signposted to Whitwell. After circulating around the garden of the house you will resume your previous direction – with magnificent views to boot!

When the hedge-lined path curves distinctly left after about 200 yards, follow the curve for a few more yards and turn right from a waymark post, crossing the field to another waymark post at the left-hand extremity of what was once an island of tall trees, now sadly demolished (100°). On arrival turn right so that the 'island' is on your immediate left and the field on your right. Walk the entire length of the 'island', and when it terminates keep straight on, crossing an open field all the way to a road and in the direction of

Cottages facing The Green at Kimpton.

Kimpton's church steeple (200°) – that's if you can spot it amongst the trees.

Keep forward from the road junction ahead, then branch right, into the churchyard path. While relaxing on a churchyard seat and enjoying the view, spare a thought for the churchyard mouse, as it climbs the seat beneath you!

Passing to the left of the church make your exit from the churchyard and follow the road (Church Lane once more) back down to Kimpton's High Street.

11 Burnham Green
The Duck

Nothing could be more appropriate to a pleasant village green than an unspoilt country pub. Here at the Duck, a homely atmosphere goes hand in hand with all that today's customers appreciate in the way of comfort and cleanliness, good ale and home-cooked food.

The lunchtime bar menu presents a wide range of snacks and main meals. There are rolls and sandwiches, omelettes, filled jacket potatoes, salads, ham and sausages. Fish, chicken and steaks come in a number of permutations and there is a good choice of vegetarian meals. The specials board adds further variety daily and the sweets menu offers several possibilities for rounding off an enjoyable meal. Food times are 12 noon to 3 pm and 7 pm to 10 pm on Monday to Saturday, and 12 noon to 7 pm on Sunday. The lunchtime bar menu is available throughout and there is a separate menu for the evenings. Families are made very welcome and can dine in the restaurant or in the garden.

There are always four to five real ales, two draught lagers and Scrumpy Jack draught cider, also an extensive selection of wines.

The pub is open 'all day' every day – 11 am to 11 pm on Monday to Saturday, and 12 noon to 10.30 pm on Sunday. Dogs may be taken into the garden – or tied up at the front!
Telephone: 01438 798358.

How to get there: The pub is very close to the green. If you are coming from the A1(M) join the A1000 from junction 6 and follow signs to Hertford at the earliest opportunity. Leave the A1000 after ½ mile for the road signposted to Digswell and turn first left into Harmer Green Road just beyond the magnificent Digswell railway viaduct. Stay in this road all the way to Burnham Green – even when it changes its name from Harmer Green Lane to New Road and back again.

Parking: At the front of the pub or alongside the green.

Length of the walk: 2¼ miles. Map: OS Landranger 166 Luton, Hertford and surrounding area (inn GR 262166).

Divided equally between fieldside paths and a tree-shaded bridleway, this walk offers fine views across Hertfordshire along the outward stretch and all the attractions of mixed woodland on the return – including some superb specimens of oak and sweet chestnut. Expect a little mud along parts of the bridleway and come prepared!

The Walk

Turn right as you leave the Duck, then immediately right into White Horse Lane, the road signposted to Knebworth. Leave the road quite soon by crossing the green in front of the White Horse pub and join a path between the pub's garage and the first of a line of houses. You may have noticed that the white horse is headless. Tradition has it that a horse was decapitated during a confrontation hereabouts in the Civil War and that at night it can be heard galloping down White Horse Lane!

The path passes to the left of an electricity sub-station and enters a field corner from a stile. After crossing the stile go into the left-hand field and continue forward, following the hedgeless field edge and eventually walking alongside a stand of trees. Continue forward with the wavering field edge all the way down to the far right-hand corner. Here you will meet up with a wood edge that

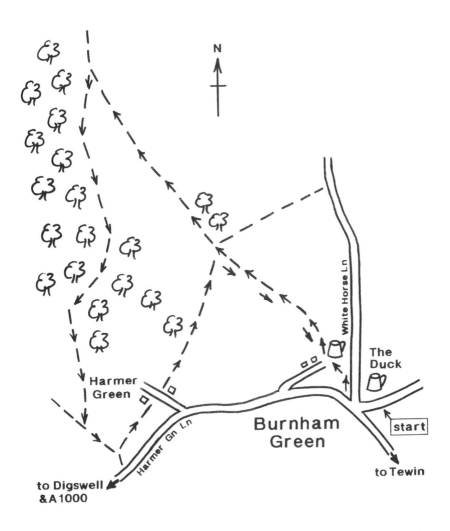

has been approaching from the left. You should also find a metal signpost.

Go forward under the trees for a few yards only and turn hairpin left into a bridleway. Follow the bridleway uphill just inside the wood and alongside a wire fence. When adjacent to a left-hand field corner at the top of the hill (there is a 'gas' marker here), keep forward with the fence, while going deeper into the wood. A number of alternative paths have been worked hereafter, doubtless to avoid mud, but these are all within the confines of two widely-spaced wire fences (210°). In due course a field comes into view on the right and the bridleway continues under the trees – which include some very fine specimens of oak and sweet chestnut and a once-layered hornbeam hedge.

Go over a raised farm crossing and continue forward to a waymarked T-junction, with paddocks and greenhouses in view ahead. Turn left here and soon arrive at a waymarked crossing under a magnificent oak tree. Turn left (with a yellow arrow) and walk behind gardens and under trees. Go over a stile and continue ahead alongside a garden fence and garage wall to a gate, then through another gate to a cul-de-sac. This passage through the property of Barneswood Lodge is surprising, but perfectly legal!

Cross the cul-de-sac to a path opposite (to the left of Butlers Cottage) and soon emerge at the corner of a meadow. Keep straight on along the left side of the meadow and enter a field from the far corner. Cross this field (which you should recognise from earlier in the walk) towards the right-hand extremity of a stand of trees and roughly in the direction of a distant church steeple. Having crossed the field, turn right and follow its left-hand edge all the way to the field corner. After leaving the field go over a stile and soon return to Burnham Green's green.

12 Tonwell
The Robin Hood and Little John

Famous over many years for the quality of its water, Tonwell (the 'village of springs') supplied this valuable product to breweries near and far. In a peaceful setting just off the A602, the village is now perhaps best known for its excellent hostelry, the Robin Hood and Little John.

Although the pub may well have been here for two centuries and more (perhaps part of the time as Ye Olde Magpie Ale House), it continues to go out of its way to attract and satisfy its customers, not least by the quality and variety of the food. This is presented on regular and blackboard menus. The former includes starters, fish dishes, filled jacket potatoes, ploughman's lunches, rolls and sweets. The blackboard adds considerable variety to this, so much so that most people will find their choice difficult to make. The full menus are in use every day from 12 noon to 2 pm and 6 pm to 9.30 pm (7 pm to 9 pm Sunday). Children are very welcome here – they have their own favourite food and there is a separate family room, which is normally a no-smoking area. If the youngsters prefer to be outside, their parents can relax in the knowledge that the patio garden is fenced and safe.

The regular real ales – Marston's Pedigree and McMullens AK – are supplemented by two guests, which are changed weekly. Strongbow cider and Stella and Carlsberg lagers are on draught. The pub is open for drinking on Monday to Saturday from 12 noon to 2.30 pm (3 pm on Saturday) and 5.30 pm to 11 pm. On Sunday the times are 12 noon to 3 pm and 7 pm to 10.30 pm. There are usually a number of special offers on both food and drink. Well-behaved dogs are welcome in the garden only.

Telephone: 01920 463352.

How to get there: Tonwell is bypassed by, and signposted from, the A602 2 miles north-west of Ware. It is also signposted where the A602 meets the B158. The pub is easily found along Tonwell's main street, Ware Road.

Parking: In the pub's own car park. You could, alternatively, park in the main street (Ware Road), especially opposite Barley Croft where the road is widest.

Length of the walk: 2 miles. Map: OS Landranger 166 Luton, Hertford and surrounding area (inn GR 333172).

Accompanied by views of the Rib valley, this easy, uncomplicated walk makes a beeline for one of Hertfordshire's most attractive small villages, Chapmore End. Here the pond with its resident ducks gives much pleasure to visitors, as does the nearby inn, the Woodman. The walk doubles back before reaching Stonyhills, and crosses cultivated fields on its return to Tonwell.

The Walk

Turning left out of the pub, go past the school (notice the old bell by the porch) to the T-junction at the main road (the A602). Cross carefully to a signpost and stile under electricity wires opposite – without confusing this with another stile to the right, out of sight along the same road. Walk downhill across an attractive meadow to a footbridge at the bottom, following power lines as you go, then continue uphill between the fields along a good path. A view of the Rib valley opens up on the left and the path joins company with a

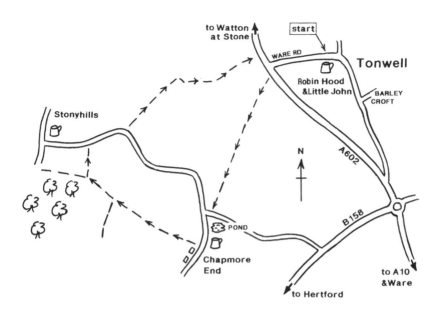

hedge (on the right). The wires go their own way and the path evolves into a grassy track, eventually meeting the road at Chapmore End. In other words it's straight on all the way from Tonwell.

Turn right into the road and left alongside the pond – a lovely place to stand and stare! After passing the Woodman pub the next manoeuvre is to join a signposted path on the right, but before doing that do enjoy Chapmore End to the full by continuing a little further along the road – at least as far as White Cottage (no 9). Returning to the footpath (a right turn if approaching from the pond and passing the Woodman), go along this, firstly alongside a garden fence, then through a gate and straight on. You will pass to the right of a line of poplar trees and a tennis court before emerging at a corner of a field.

Continue forward, but now along the field edge (there is a hedge on your immediate right), aiming for the right-hand extremity of a wood ahead. Ignore a bridleway coming in from the left as you go, and turn right when you finally arrive at the wood corner. A glance half-left across this next field will give you sight of the Three Harts at Stonyhills. Follow the hedge to a road and turn right (left for the

61

A classic village pond at Chapmore End.

Three Harts) and when the road itself turns right keep forward on a level path across the fields (50°), passing an electricity pole near the start. The cone-shaped water tower at Tonwell eventually comes into view, slightly right, before the path turns right.

Go right with the path and bear left when you soon (35 yards) strike a hedge corner. Now it's simply a matter of following the hedge as it winds its way to the A602, with the water tower as your point of aim. As you walk that final stretch you may catch sight of the large but distant house among the trees half-left. This is Sacombe House – built around 1805 but too far away from here to appreciate!

Cross the A602 to Ware Road opposite and soon find yourself back at the Robin Hood and Little John.

13 Widford
The Green Man

Widford is closely associated with the author and essayist Charles Lamb, who lodged in the village on many occasions and often frequented the Bell, Widford's other pub. Visitors and local residents are as delighted with the Green Man today as Lamb apparently was with the Bell in his day. Where food is concerned the Green Man has exemplary aims – to satisfy the inner man without harming his pocket.

The fare is simple but sustaining and nicely presented. Choices range from sandwiches through to sirloin steak and include omelettes, fish (scampi, plaice and cod), steak and kidney pie, sausages and burgers. There is an 'all day breakfast', with no less than eight items, and a variety of specials and sweets. If you crave something that is not on the blackboard at the time of your visit, you are invited to make your wishes known. And if you are self-sufficient in food, you may eat this in the attractive orchard-style garden, as long as you are buying drinks. Children are very welcome here, inside or out. For those whose ages are measured in

Thatched cottage in Widford.

months rather than years, a bottle warming service is offered! Well-behaved dogs may accompany you into the bar or the garden. Real ales number about five, and include Gladstone, a McMullen innovation. Foster's and Stella lagers are on draught, also Strongbow cider and Guinness. The food hours and opening times are one and the same – 11 am to 11 pm on Monday to Saturday, and 12 noon to 10.30 pm on Sunday.

Telephone: 01279 842454.

How to get there: The Green Man is easily found – in Widford's High Street on the B1004 between Much Hadham and Ware.

Parking: In the pub's car park or along Hunsdon Road (the B180) nearby.

Length of the walk: 2½ miles. Map: OS Landranger 167 Chelmsford, Harlow and surrounding area (inn GR 420159).

After a short introduction through fieldside and meadow, the walk joins Nether Street, a quiet lane and retreat of country cottages. It enjoys the heady heights of cultivated fields before descending to the B1004 and the Ash, and follows the river for ½ mile prior to climbing a short steep hill back into Widford.

The Walk

Turn right on leaving the Green Man and branch left into the B180 Hunsdon Road. Leave this very soon along a signposted footpath on the left – just beyond a large metal barn and opposite the B1004 road sign. When this path crosses a farm drive keep forward alongside a hedge to a field corner. On approaching a single-storey brick building after 60 yards, turn left from a waymark post. Follow the field edge, with a hedge on the left, as it gradually curves right, then cross a stile on the left where the field edge goes briefly, but sharply, right. Keep straight on from the stile, across a meadow to another stile and a road (Nether Street).

Looking left along Nether Street you have sight of a lovely cottage terrace, and beyond that a thatched house. Turn right into the road and, passing yet more desirable habitations, follow it to where the tarmac ceases. Go half-left here along what is signposted as a bridleway (Nether Street continues as a 'Byway') and follow a

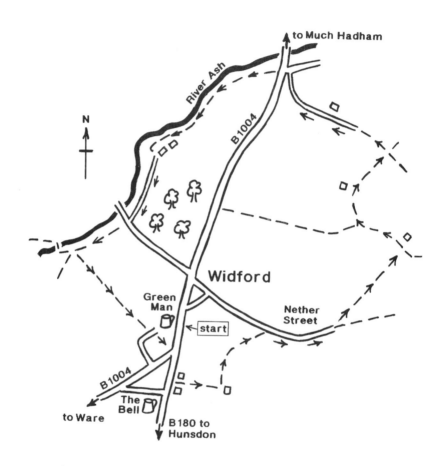

row of telephone poles between the fields. Go through a gap at the far end and emerge by a waymark post opposite the entrance to a bungalow. Turn left into a rough drive and, when this turns right, ignore a bridleway entering trees on the left.

Staying in the drive and following its sweeping right-hand curve, pass the entrance to Phoenix Farm and eventually arrive at a crossing. There is a cattle grid here and a pair of entrance piers that seem calculated to impress. Turn left at the crossing along a rough drive, passing between hedges and alongside Mill Park Lodge, then stay the course all the way down to a road (Bourne Lane). Turn left into Bourne Lane and soon cross the B1004 to the left-hand of two fields. There is a bridleway sign here and a bus stop nearby.

Nether Street, Widford.

Enter the field at its corner and follow the right-hand edge. The river Ash comes into view in places through the trees before the field gives way to Hadham Mill Pumping Station. Pass to the right of the pumping station, between fences and soon join the concrete entrance drive. Turn right into the drive and stay with it as far as a crossing. Although your next move is straight on along a fenced path, a short diversion along the lane to your right is all that is required for a good view of the river.

Back at the crossing, follow the path between fields, then under trees (with the river alongside) to where it turns left. There are two stiles here. The one on the right leads into a meadow and shortly to a footbridge – for another pleasant encounter with the river. The left-hand stile is the one we want and connects with a steeply sloping meadow. Walk the raised path uphill through the meadow, aiming at a rooftop on the summit (140°). After following a short fence (on your right) cross a stile and walk a narrow path, eventually passing between gardens to a cul-de-sac.

Turn left in the cul-de-sac and cross to a tarmac path between the houses. Ignore an opening to a small car park and soon arrive at the B1004 near the Green Man.

14 Lilley
The Lilley Arms

Well away from the busy A505, the Lilley Arms is situated in what is arguably one of Hertfordshire's most attractive and desirable retreats. A brochure introduces the pub as a 300 year old coaching inn and an early photograph on display in the bar shows a coach drawn up outside what was then called the Sowerby Arms. Today the hostelry has a wide appeal, and not least to the children. They will certainly enjoy the garden, where they can watch the hens, ducks and goats and Bertie, the pot-bellied pig! – Children are also welcome in the dining room (which is usually smoke-free) or in the pool room.

There are separate menus for weekdays and Sundays, each with very extensive choices. During the week there are starters, hot dishes, salad platters, omelettes, sandwiches and sweets. On Sundays the omelettes and sandwiches give way to a wider selection of hot dishes (including vegetarian food and a roast) while the starters, salad platters and sweets remain. Children have their own special menu, and take-away food is available for those who prefer to eat al fresco. Meals are served every day from 12 noon to 2.15 pm (ish) and 7 pm to 9.30 pm, but not on Sunday evenings.

The real ales are Greene King IPA and Abbot Ale. Blackthorn Dry cider is on draught, also Harp and Kronenbourg lagers. There is a choice of wines to appeal to all tastes. Opening hours are from 11.30 am to 3 pm and 5.30 pm to 11 pm on Monday to Friday, 11.30 am to 11 pm on Saturday, and 12 noon to 10.30 pm on Sunday. For a longer stay, bed and breakfast accommodation is provided in twin, double and family rooms. Dogs on leads are welcome in the bar area. If taken into the garden, due consideration should be given to all the resident animals!

Telephone: 01462 768371.

How to get there: Lilley is signposted from the A505 between Luton and Hitchin. If approaching that way, branch left into a 'no through road' immediately after passing the parish church. The pub will be found on the left side of the road. Bus service 92–99 between Luton and Hitchin calls at Lilley half-hourly on Monday to Saturday. There is a frequent rail service from London (Kings Cross) to Hitchin and from London (Thameslink) to Luton.

Parking: In the pub's own car park or along the roadside nearby.

Length of the walk: 2½ miles. Map: OS Landranger 166 Luton, Hertford and surrounding area (inn GR 117265).

After traversing level pastures parallel to Lilley's main street the walk rises to the heights of Lilley Hoo, where it enjoys an invigorating expanse of woodland and cultivated fields – and the subsequent steep descent is blessed with a view that will make your day complete!

The Walk

Turn right on leaving the Lilley Arms, then left into the main street from the small triangular green. You will not fail to notice the rampant lion crests on many of the houses. This is often referred to as the Docwra Crest after Thomas Docwra, Lord of the Manor of Lilley in the 16th century. Look for a bridleway sign on the right opposite Wayside and go along the rough drive, passing to the left of a garage at the start. The drive narrows to a path beyond the last

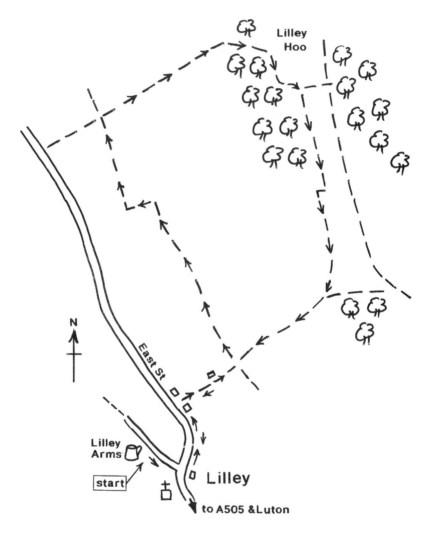

house and descends the hill between hedges. At a three-way signpost near the bottom of the valley, leave the path by turning left into the lowest field at its corner. Follow the left-hand edge of this field and the next, and on arrival at the far end of the second field (beyond an electricity pole) go over a stile and turn left.

Follow a hedge on your left and soon turn right from the field corner. Resuming your previous direction, parallel to the valley,

West Street, Lilley.

walk a field edge track to the far left-hand corner. Make your exit through a gap there and turn right immediately at a crossing of ways, then descend the gentle slope along a wide, hedge-bordered, grassy swathe. After dipping into a shallow valley keep forward and go uphill through a gap and into a wood. On emerging from the wood at the top (where you may find a signpost pointing to Lilley) turn right and follow the waverings of the wood edge (and the field edge) until it goes into the straight. Ignore a path crossing the field at this point and stay with the straight wood edge until it gives way to a hedge (170°).

The hedge diverts briefly to the right before resuming its previous direction, finally taking you to a small, uncultivated area of grass (and a waymark post) beyond the field's far right-hand corner. After turning right you now have the pleasant task of descending the steep hill and enjoying the magnificent view ahead. Once in the dip continue forward and soon arrive back at Lilley. Turn left in the road there and first right for the Lilley Arms.

15 Preston
The Red Lion

The Red Lion has the distinction of being the first pub in England to be owned by the local community – and judging by the way Preston's residents care for their attractive village, they are going to be equally caring for their one and only hostelry. The atmosphere of the bars and the choices in food and drink epitomise all that a village inn should be – to the obvious satisfaction of those who enter.

'Sue's Home Made Fayre' includes a good variety of hot meals – farmer's steak, ham off the bone, vegetarian lasagne, cod in batter, and much more. There is an unusual range of ploughman's lunches, also filled jacket potatoes and crusty rolls, toasted sandwiches and sweets. All this and a choice of specials every day from 12 noon to 2.30 pm and 7 pm to 9.30 pm.

Some interesting labels appear on the real ale handpumps, of which there are five in number (four and a guest). Cidermaster Dry is on draught, also Stella and Carling lagers. Drinking hours are from 12 noon to 3 pm and 5.30 pm to 11 pm on Monday to Friday,

12 noon to 11 pm on Saturday, and 12 noon to 3 pm and 7 pm to 10.30 pm on Sunday. Children are welcome in the Snug Bar. If the weather is kind, the beautifully maintained garden, with its colourful flowerbeds and its petanque pitches, is a very nice place to be. You may eat your own food there, when buying drinks. If you are leading a large party of walkers, prior warning of your visit would be appreciated. Dogs are allowed inside and out, if kept on leads.

Telephone: 01462 459585.

How to get there: Preston is signposted from the B651 south of Hitchin. It can also be approached from Great Offley near the A505 south-west of Hitchin, initially following signs to King's Walden, but this is a long country route. On arrival at Preston the pub is easily found – it overlooks the green at the centre of the village.

Parking: In the pub's own car park. Roadside parking is possible but limited; you could try Church Lane where the road is widest.

Length of the walk: 3½ miles. Map: OS Landranger 166 Luton, Hertford and surrounding area (inn GR 180247).

Almost the whole spectrum of Hertfordshire's countryside is presented in this walk – meadow and cultivated field, woodland and hedgerow, ancient cottage and farmstead, footpath, bridleway and byway – all within the framework of an undulating landscape. This variety in landscape can mean variety in the 'going', so be prepared for some mud, especially after rain.

The Walk

Turn left as you leave the pub and go along the 'no through road' to a metalled path between fences. When the path meets a road, turn left and, passing the primary school, continue to a small triangular green at a road junction. Keep straight on here along a quiet lane and look for a footpath signpost on the right where the lane is at its lowest point. Go over the stile there and enter a rough pasture. Walk the left edge of the pasture alongside a hedge to the far left-hand corner and continue forward in similar fashion along the next two fields. Now hold it there!

Go along the third field for 50 yards only – to a waymarked gap

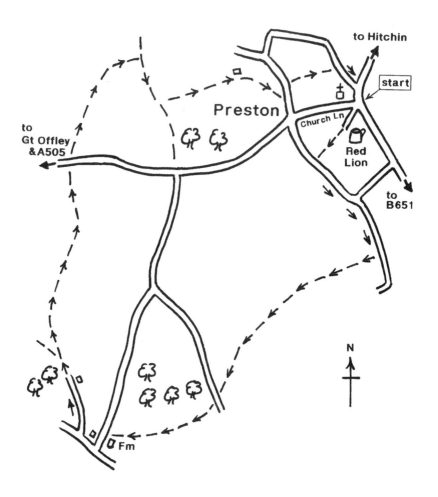

on the left. Turn half-left through the gap and cross the adjacent field to a point 50 yards left of a distant wood (210°). If your eyesight is good you will see a metal signpost by the lane there! (If you make the mistake of walking the whole length of the third field, you will need to turn left into the lane at the end.) Cross the lane to a stile opposite and go uphill in a field at right angles to the lane (260°). The path runs parallel to the wood edge and, if you look back, provides one of the county's best views. On arrival at the summit cross a farmyard – passing to the right of an open barn – and join another lane.

Turn left in the lane and right after about 40 yards at a road junction (for King's Walden). After passing a farmhouse, turn right into a 'no through road' (there is a postbox here). The lane evolves into a track beyond the last pair of houses and a path (which you should ignore) in due course branches from the left. At this point a sign pronounces the track a 'Public Byway', so if you see wheeled traffic along here (anything from bicycles upwards) don't be too surprised! The track narrows and curves right between hedges and fields. It descends to a dip and rises to join a road beyond a stand of tall oak trees.

Cross the road to the good track opposite (labelled as a bridleway) and stay with this for ⅓ mile alongside the fields to a T-junction at the summit. Turn right at the T-junction into the track under trees and go downhill to a stile on the left. The stile is about 75 yards prior to the corner of the wood ahead and connects with an undulating field. Cross the field to a waymarked gate in the top left-hand corner, then continue in the same direction in the next field, aiming towards a single-storey brick-built barn (70°). Turn half-right on passing between this and a cattle shelter and cross the centre of a pasture to a stile on the far side – to the left of a tall sycamore tree (110°).

The stile (which you will not see until you are close to it) gives access to a road, where you should turn left. Leave the road after only 30 yards and join a narrow path on the right beyond The Willows. This path runs into a small pasture, in which you should keep straight on. Another path soon takes over and leads you forward to a road (Chequers Lane). Turn right here and right again for the pub.

16 Walkern
The Yew Tree

Villages that can support as many as three pubs must today be considered unusual, if not a rarity. Walkern's success is doubtless due to its location – along a B road busy with tradesmen and casual visitors. The High Street is an attraction in its own right – humble well-kept cottages contrasting markedly with the grandeur of Manor Farm and its fine dovecote.

The Yew Tree is also an attraction – for the sincerity of its welcome and the quality of its food and drink. Stand near the bar for a while and see how nicely prepared the dishes are, as they are rushed to the waiting customers. The lunchtime snack and grill menu (available every day) offers an impressive variety of sandwiches, filled jacket potatoes, omelettes and burgers. Specials on the blackboard are likely to include steak and kidney pie, cod in batter, vegetarian Kiev and beef stir-fry. 'Children's Choices' encompass 'all that kiddies like' and the sweets menu will start you drooling at the mouth.

There are usually no less than five real ales, including a Special

Reserve from McMullen. This is an old ale revived – in the best sense of the word of course! Foster's, Stella Artois and Hartsman lagers are on draught, also Strongbow cider. Food and drink are available from 12 noon to 3 pm and 6 pm to 11 pm on Monday to Friday (food until 10 pm), 12 noon to 11 pm on Saturday (food until 10 pm), and 12 noon to 2.30 pm on Sunday. On Sunday evening the pub is open from 7 pm to 10.30 pm, but for drinking only. Children are always very welcome inside, or outside in the patio garden. Dogs should be kept on leads and away from the eating area.
Telephone: 01438 861321.

How to get there: The Yew Tree is easily found along Walkern's High Street (the B1037) a few miles east of Stevenage.

Parking: In the pub's car park or along the roadside nearby. You could, alternatively, park in Church End near the northern end of the High Street.

Length of the walk: 2¼ miles. Map: OS Landranger 166 Luton, Hertford and surrounding area (inn GR 289263).

After leaving Walkern's High Street, the walk makes straight for the parish church, where, in the purist of tones, the clock marks each quarter-hour. The river Beane is forded (footbridge provided!) and the walk continues – across undulating fields and alongside woodland, finally recrossing the Beane and returning to the High Street.

The Walk
Turning right from the Yew Tree, walk the High Street as far as the next pub, the White Lion. Cross a stile just beyond this pub's car park and go along a short path to another stile. If the 'bull in field' notice on the second stile causes some concern you should return to the High Street, turn right there and right again into Church End. We'll catch up with you by the ford along Church End! Chances are you will see no bull in the field and can cross it in peace, while aiming for the right-hand end of a long grey barn. As you cross the field, glance back for a view of the very fine dovecote at Manor Farm. Turn left around the barn and, passing other outbuildings,

The Dovecote, Walkern.

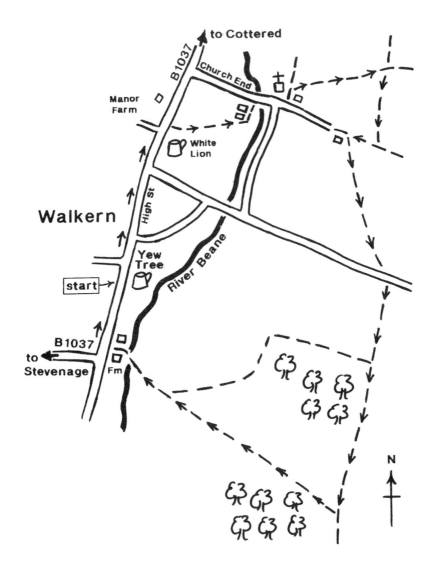

soon cross a stile and join Church End.

After turning right and crossing the ford, keep straight on at a road junction, soon leaving the road for a footpath on the left. This is just beyond the churchyard and leads to a stile and a field. Cross the field half-right to its distant corner, passing a pond near that corner and going over a stile. Walk briefly under the trees –

between one waymark post and another – and turn right into a shady path between the trees and a field edge. On meeting a track at a T-junction, turn right and stay with the track for about 60 yards to a footpath signpost on the left, prior to a pair of semi-detached houses. Cross the field here, slightly uphill along a raised path.

On meeting a lane on the far side of the field, turn left and, after a few yards, right into a farm track labelled as a bridleway. This good track takes you into a dip and uphill alongside a wood. Stay with the track in the next field, but for 150 yards only, as far as a hedge gap on the right. The track is still climbing (very slightly) just here and a waymark arrow points through the gap to a wood corner. Obeying the arrow, turn sharp right from the track and cross a field (300°), clipping the wood corner and descending the hill in the direction of two black barns sited in the valley bottom. After crossing a footbridge enter the next field and continue straight on downhill.

When the path levels out keep straight on, not along the farm track but across the field, cutting off a large corner. After crossing the river Beane go through the farmyard (Finche's Farm) and soon join the B1037, turning right there for the Yew Tree.

17 Standon
The Star

With the Roman highways Ermine Street and Stane Street meeting nearby and the river Rib flowing through and driving the mills, it is no surprise that Standon evolved into a thriving market town. Today the High Street is almost a haven of quietness, and retains many fine buildings from those early times. Set among them is the Star public house, a haven of another kind – for those seeking refreshment in an atmosphere of old world charm.

The menu at the Star includes many of the established favourites – steaks, curries, quiches, plaice, scampi, salads and ploughman's lunches – and what is by all accounts 'the best pork chop in Hertfordshire!' And when the line-up of sweets includes toffee apple crunch, hot chocolate fudge cake and home-made apple pie, you could hardly be in a happier place. These delights can be enjoyed on Monday to Saturday from 12 noon to 2.30 pm and on Wednesday to Saturday evenings from 7 pm to 9.30 pm. If you would like food at Sunday lunchtime you could call instead at the Heron on the A120 nearby. You could, alternatively, bring your own food and eat this in the garden, but only if buying drinks. As a further Sunday option (for walking parties and family groups) meals can be ordered in advance, giving at least one day's notice.

Greene King IPA and Abbot Ale are on draught, also Kronenbourg and Harp lagers and Dry Blackthorn cider. Opening hours are from 12 noon to 2.30 pm and 6 pm to 11 pm on Monday to Saturday, and 12 noon to 3 pm and 7 pm to 10.30 pm on Sunday. Children are very welcome and can be taken into the dining area. The secluded garden has swings, a slide and two petanque pitches. Dogs are allowed in the bar or the garden, but only if kept well at heel.

Telephone: 01920 821258.

How to get there: If approaching from the A10(T), join the A120 midway between Ware and Buntingford. After crossing the river Rib at Standon, turn right into the High Street. You will find the Star directly opposite the parish church.

Parking: In the pub's car park or along the wide High Street.

Length of the walk: 2 miles. Map: OS Landranger 166 Luton, Hertford and surrounding area (inn GR 396223).

Uncomplicated and very nearly level, this walk follows the lovely river Rib through sheep pastures towards and beyond the Lordship, a manor house with 16th-century origins. After crossing the river, the walk returns to Standon alongside the route of the long-gone Ware, Hadham and Buntingford Railway. A gem of a walk if ever there was!

The Walk

Turn right on leaving the Star (first right after crossing the river, if starting at the Heron) and walk along the High Street as far as its junction with Paper Mill Lane. The chunk of Hertfordshire puddingstone on the little green here once functioned as a mounting block (getting on and off your horse!) and was located in the churchyard wall nearby. The impressive timber-framed building opposite served part of its time as the village school, and before that as the Hospice of the Knights of St John – or so it is thought.

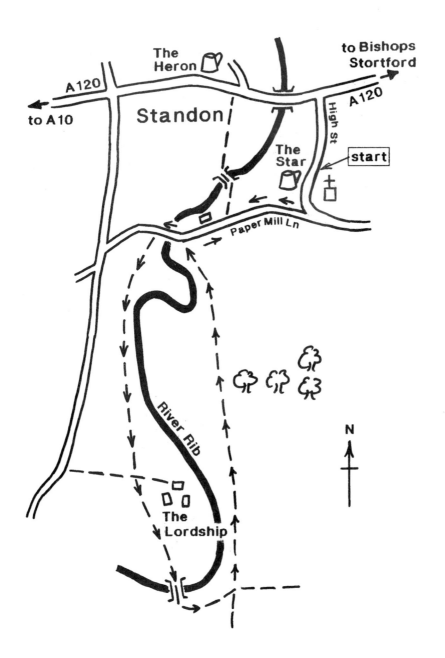

The river Rib.

Turn hairpin right into Paper Mill Lane and follow this straight on towards the river Rib. A hump in the road well before the river marks the line of the former Ware, Hadham and Buntingford railway, which was closed in 1964 after 101 years of service. Closer to the river is Paper Mill House. The fine paper required for bibles was for many years manufactured at the watermill here. By descending to the riverside 'beach' you can view the site of the mill workings.

Cross the river by the footbridge and shortly go through a gate on the left. There is a footpath signpost at this point and the road surface returns to tarmac. The path through the meadow may not be clearly marked, but you should aim for the far end of a forward-going hedge (200°). Subsequently keeping to the lowest level of the meadow – with the river meandering along its course to your left – you will come in sight of the one-time manor of Standon Lordship, dating back to 1546 and now known simply as the Lordship.

After a gentle climb across the centre of the meadow, the path (such as it is) meets a waymarked stile and gate at the end. From the stile soon cross a metalled drive (leading to the Lordship) and keep straight on across the grass and through a gate. Bear slightly left with a field track and in due course pass under hawthorn trees (from a farm gate) and cross the river. Turn left immediately beyond the river and stay with the hedged track for 150 yards until you see a pair of waymarked gates on the left. This is a short distance (30 yards) before the crossing of power lines.

Having entered the meadow on the left, soon follow those power lines, with the river downhill on the left and a superb view of the Lordship beyond that. The terraced field edge on your immediate right is another sad reminder of the Ware to Buntingford railway, heading towards Standon. Keep straight on beyond another pair of gates, and, following the power lines and the right-hand fence, make your exit from the meadow via a gate in the far right-hand corner.

Turning right into Paper Mill Lane, you could simply follow this all the way to the puddingstone and turn left for the Star. For a little light relief however – and another good sighting of the river – leave the lane at the hump (the old railway crossing) and go along a short stretch of trackbed on the left. If destined for the Heron, you could cross the river and follow the right-hand edge of a meadow all the way to the A120 and the pub. For the Star, return to Paper Mill Lane from the river and turn left.

18 Chipping
The Countryman

'1663' above the fireplace in the bar of the Countryman leaves us in little doubt as to the age of this marvellous old pub. The road that it overlooks (the A10) goes back very much further, for this is none other than the Roman Ermine Street. The pub shares a short piece of Ermine Street with the imposing Chipping Hall and with the river Rib which passes nearby.

A highlight of the menu is the giant Yorkshire pudding, with a choice of around 10 different fillings. Other hot meals include fish, steaks, curries and stir-fries. Under the 'Cold Snacks' heading are sandwiches and ploughman's lunches, together with the plough-man's close relatives the 'Countryman' and the 'Trawlerman'. There are some very nice desserts to round off the meal, which could be followed by a cup of freshly ground coffee. Food is available every day from 12 noon to 3 pm and 7 pm to 9.30 pm (6.30 pm start on Saturday) but not on Sunday evenings.

About five real ales and four draught lagers are on offer, and a 'good cellar' of wines. The pub is open every day from 12 noon to

11 pm (10.30 pm on Sunday). In winter you can enjoy your food and drink while basking in the comfort of a real log fire. In summer you may prefer to be in the garden, which is without question one of the most attractive pub gardens in the county. Children are made very welcome and can be taken into the bar-free dining room, that's if they haven't already opted for the superb Wendy house outside! Dogs are allowed in the garden only, if kept on leads.

Telephone: 01763 272721.

How to get there: Chipping and the Countryman are easily found on the A10 between Buntingford and Royston.

Parking: In the pub's car park. You are welcome to leave your car there before the pub opens – assuming you are a prospective customer! Parking on the A10 is not advised, but you may feel happy to leave your car in The Square. This is north of the pub and a short distance beyond the telephone box.

Length of the walk: 2½ miles. Map: OS Landranger 166 Luton, Hertford and surrounding area (inn GR 356320).

A walk that is the ultimate in simplicity. It takes a steady but not-too-demanding incline along a farm track to Capons Wood. It skirts the wood, crosses a field and comes back down again! As an introduction to the wide-sweeping landscape of north-east Hertfordshire, this is hard to beat.

The Walk

Turn right from the Countryman and soon cross the river Rib where it passes under the A10. Join a wide track on the right (signposted as a bridleway to Wyddial) immediately beyond the river and follow this up past Brook Cottage. From here the track gradually ascends the hill – between fields and with a hedge on the right initially. After ½ mile and close to a wood at the top it turns left towards the wood corner. Although the track itself continues forward from the corner, you should take your leave of it by turning right into a level, grassy path, placing the wood on your immediate left.

When the wood edge terminates at the next corner continue forward over a footbridge and cross a field straight on to a track on

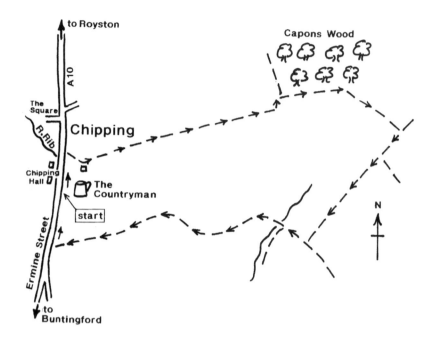

the opposite side (130°). Turn right into the track, and, with a hedge on your left, continue ahead, ignoring a branch leaving from the left (for Wyddial) as you go. When the track turns right after ⅓ mile (having previously parted company with the hedge) go with it into a dip where the fields meet. Cross the ditch here (the main track turns left and goes its own way) and climb a grassy track as it bears slightly left.

On reaching the summit the track is joined by a hedge, from where it wends its way downhill to the A10. The church tower at Buckland (1½ miles) comes into view on the right as you descend, while the impressive front of Chipping Hall appears directly ahead. On arrival at the A10 turn right and soon find yourself at the Countryman.

An uncomplicated walk if ever there was!

19 Brent Pelham
The Black Horse Inn

Piers Shonks, a medieval Lord of the Manor, is at the centre of a tradition that has held fast here for centuries. The saying goes that this 'giant of a man' slew a dragon in the forest and is buried within the north wall of Brent Pelham church. His tomb is no myth, however, and is there for all to see. Down the hill from the church is the much-acclaimed Black Horse Inn, in a delightfully rural setting. With its large terraced garden backed by tall trees this is a marvellous place in which to spend a summer lunch break. In winter the comfort of the real log fires more than compensates for the cold outside.

All the food choices are 'on the blackboard'. They include starters, main meals and a wide selection of salads and ploughman's lunches. Cod, plaice, skate and scampi are all offered, and examples of other hot dishes are chicken with garlic, Stilton, mushroom and pasta bake and ham, egg and chips. Meals are served every day from 12 noon to 2 pm and 7 pm to 9.30 pm. At Sunday lunchtime the main meals are replaced by a variety of roasts, while the salads and ploughman's are available as usual.

The real ales are Greene King IPA and Courage Directors. Red Rock cider is on draught, also Kronenbourg and Castlemaine XXXX lagers. The inn is open for drinking from 12 noon to 3 pm and 5.30 pm to 11 pm on Monday to Friday, 12 noon to 11 pm on Saturday, and 12 noon to 3 pm and 7 pm to 10.30 pm on Sunday. Children are welcome in the dining room. Dogs may be taken into the bar area or the garden, but their owners may wish to know that there are four cats in residence!

Telephone: 01279 777305.

How to get there: Brent Pelham is on the B1038 4½ miles east of Buntingford, from where it is signposted. On arrival at Brent Pelham turn left (if driving from Buntingford) by the war memorial and parish church; you will find the Black Horse Inn at the bottom of the hill.

Parking: In the inn's large car park or along the roadside a very short distance into the walk. You could, alternatively, park opposite the church at the top of the hill.

Length of the walk: 2½ miles. Map: OS Landranger 167 Chelmsford, Harlow and surrounding area (inn GR 433310).

Requiring little in the way of vigour, this walk circulates around an area of arable farmland, which is punctuated by well-maintained hedgerows and woodland. It passes within good viewing distance of two fine 17th-century houses, Brent Pelham Hall and Beeches.

The Walk

On leaving the pub's entrance drive turn left in the road and go uphill to the first bridleway on the left (you may have parked your car at this point or further on opposite the church). Go through the gate here and walk the short track under trees to another gate. This gives access to a pasture which you should cross more or less straight on, with Brent Pelham Hall in view to your right. Keeping parallel to the edge of the pasture, aim for another gate near the far right corner, adjacent to the right-hand extremity of a wood (70°). There are cattle troughs and a pair of wooden electricity poles at that point.

Keep forward from the gate by following the short wood edge,

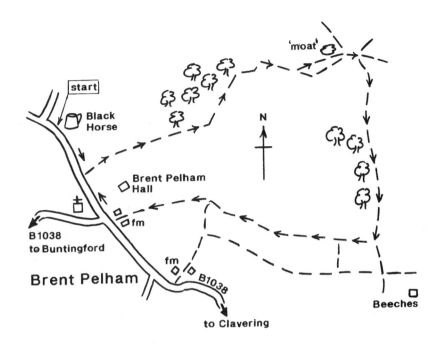

then go ahead between fields and with a wire fence on the left. On arrival at the far left-hand field corner, enter the next field and turn half-left. Follow the field edge, with a hedge on the left, until you see a gate and a gap on the left. Go through the gap (not the gate) and turn right into a track, following this alongside a ditch and hedge.

When another track comes in from the right, continue forward along the left side of a stand of oak trees. You will soon pass to the right of a mound surrounded by a water-filled moat. This is not an ancient burial site as you might suspect, but an earth mound raised by the landowner in recent years.

Just beyond the moat you will meet a good track coming in from the left. Go through a gap on the right here and turn left to resume your previous direction. Follow the short stretch (50 yards) of hedge on the left and enter the field ahead. Turn right and follow the waverings of the field edge (180° initially), with a hedge and ditch on the right, aiming for the left edge of a wood. Ignore turnings running into the wood and keep straight on, with the wood on your immediate right. Beeches, a fine 17th-century manor

Church Cottage, Brent Pelham.

house with large chimneys, comes into view ahead.

Where the wood terminates keep forward between hedges along a wide track – but for 120 yards only – to the second hedge gap on the right. If you find yourself at a crossing-track, you have walked too far (although that's a good point from which to view Beeches). Go through the gap (over an earth-filled ditch) and cross a field towards an electricity pole near the far side. Enter the next field via a wide footbridge (more correctly a 'bridlebridge'!) and continue straight ahead along a farm track, following overhead wires.

When the track turns left on its way to Down Hall Farm, go briefly right before a deep ditch and follow this round, resuming your previous direction but into a hedge-lined way (Cut Throat Lane). When you see a large pond on the right you will understand why the adjacent piece of track is in a perpetual state of muddiness. Help is at hand however, with a raised bank between the track and the pond functioning as a bypass.

Continuing along the track, soon pass through the yard of Hall Farm and emerge at a road. Turn right and go downhill to the Black Horse.

Hinxworth
The Three Horseshoes

In this, Hertfordshire's most northerly village, the thatched Three Horseshoes pub completes the canvas of an unforgettable rural scene. Inside, the pub is beautifully furnished and maintained – a real credit to the management!

On the food front the wide range takes up no less than five blackboards. The main blackboard includes hot dishes, jacket potatoes, ploughman's lunches and sandwiches. 'Happy Pig' sausages come as pork and apple or chilli and garlic and can be accompanied by chips, French bread or mash and gravy. Children's choices occupy another blackboard, balti dishes another, sweets another. On Thursdays 'over 55s' can take advantage of some special offers on meals. The Sunday blackboard offers a good variety of starters, main courses and sweets (sandwiches, jacket potatoes and ploughman's are not available on that day). Food is served daily from 12 noon to 2 pm and 7 pm to 9.30 pm, but not on Sunday evening.

There is a choice of three real ales and three draught lagers. Dry

Blackthorn cider is also on draught. Opening hours are 11.30 am to 2.30 pm and 5.30 pm to 11 pm on Monday to Friday. At weekends the opening hours are flexible, but generally 'all day' during the summer months. Children are very welcome inside and can be taken into the Top Restaurant. In the garden they will have the opportunity to meet Kevin, the pot-bellied pig! Dogs may only join you in the garden.

Telephone: 01462 742280.

How to get there: Hinxworth is clearly signposted from the A1(T) midway between Baldock and Biggleswade (Beds). The Three Horseshoes is easily found in Hinxworth's High Street.

Parking: In the pub's small car park or along the roadside nearby. It would also be convenient to park at the far end of Chapel Street, a short distance into the walk.

Length of the walk: 2¾ miles. Map: OS Landranger 153 Bedford, Huntingdon and surrounding area (inn GR 235405).

Tear yourself away from this lovely village and enjoy the wide open spaces of Hertfordshire, with views towards Ashwell and Newnham Hill that will gladden your heart! Enjoy also a singular jewel along this level, uncomplicated walk – Hinxworth Place, a unique 15th-century manor house.

The Walk

Turn left from the forecourt of the Three Horseshoes and immediately right into Chapel Street. Walk to the far end of this marvellous street and turn right at the T-junction into a rough drive. Bear left with the drive beyond a pair of semi-detached houses and soon pass between two cottages (Hillside Cottage and one other). Ashwell and its church 'spike' can then be seen directly ahead as you enter the open fields along a wide track. This sizeable village is 2 miles from here and is well worth a visit for its attractiveness and historic interest. On your way home perhaps!

The wide track runs straight and true for ½ mile, crossing a drainage ditch at the midway point and terminating on a concrete hard-standing. There are two large barns nearby (half-left). Turn right at the hard-standing into another wide track and follow this

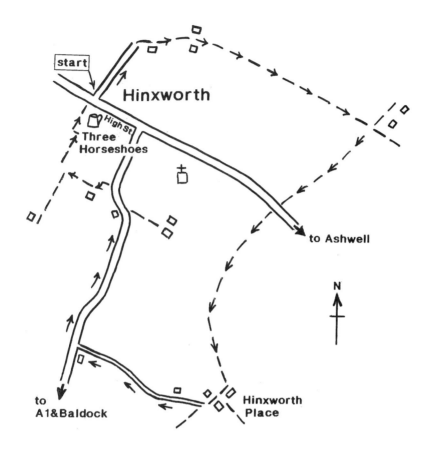

for ¼ mile between fields to a pair of gates and the Hinxworth road, with Hinxworth church in view as you proceed.

Cross to the footpath opposite (signposted to Hinxworth Place and Caldecote) and walk at right angles to the road along the left side of a row of trees, with fields to the left and right. From the end of the tree-line (where a hedge goes off to the right) strike ¼-left across the field towards a point midway between a long, low barn and the rooftop of what you will soon discover is Hinxworth Place (190°). On arrival at a hedge corner continue forward a further 30 yards to a gate, then forward again along a farm track between Hinxworth Place and a stable block. Hinxworth Place is thought to be one of the best preserved stone manor houses in Hertfordshire.

Corner Cottage Hinxworth.

It was built in the 1400s with chalk stone quarried locally. Notice in particular the very fine doorway.

After passing the house turn half-right onto the fenced drive and follow this straight through to a road. Turn right and stay with the road round an S-bend followed by a left bend opposite the entrance to Dewmead Farm – from where an interesting pantiled roof-scape on a nearby cottage can be seen. Leave the road when it soon turns right (the completion of another S-bend) and join a drive on the left by Glebe Farm Cottages. This is signposted as a footpath and takes you to the forecourt of Thorn's Farm (a farm shop).

Passing to the right of the shop go along the partly-metalled drive to where it turns left. Leave the drive here by crossing the grass and entering the field ahead. Turn right and walk the field edge to the corner, then keep forward along a fenced path, with houses and their gardens in view ahead. Don't enter the gardens but turn left and soon right, passing between the gardens to the road at Hinxworth. You will find the pub just a few yards to the right.